# THE *Rhode Island* COLONY

SPIRIT
of America®

THE *Rhode Island* COLONY

By Barbara A. Somervill

Content Adviser: Marla Miller, Ph.D. Director, Public History Program,
University of Massachusetts, Boston, Massachusetts

The Child's World®
Chanhassen, Minnesota

8

# THE *Rhode Island* COLONY

*Published in the United States of America by The Child's World®*
PO Box 326 • Chanhassen, MN 55317-0326 • 800-599-READ • www.childsworld.com

*Acknowledgments*
The Child's World®: Mary Berendes, Publishing Director

Editorial Directions, Inc.: E. Russell Primm, Editorial Director; Melissa McDaniel, Line Editor; Elizabeth K. Martin, Assistant Editor; Olivia Nellums, Editorial Assistant; Susan Hindman, Copy Editor; Joanne Mattern, Proofreader; Kevin Cunningham, Peter Garnham, Ruthanne Swiatkowski, Fact Checkers; Tim Griffin/IndexServ, Indexer; Cian Loughlin O'Day, Photo Researcher; Linda S. Koutris, Photo Selector

*Photo*
Cover: North Wind Picture Archives; Archivo Iconografico, S.A./Corbis: 7, 13; Bettmann/Corbis: 6, 14, 15, 17, 19, 21, 23, 28; Corbis: 8 (David H. Wells), 11 (Geoffrey Clements), 12 (Richard T. Nowitz), 24 (David Muench); Getty Images/Hulton Archive: 9, 20, 25, 27, 29, 31, 33, 35; Lee Snider; Lee Snider/Corbis: 18, 22, 34; North Wind Picture Archives: 30; Stock Montage: 10, 26.

*Registration*
The Child's World®, Spirit of America®, and their associated logos are the sole property and registered trademarks of The Child's World®.

*Library of Congress Cataloging-in-Publication Data*
Somervill, Barbara A.
  The Rhode Island Colony / by Barbara A. Somervill.
    p. cm. — (Our colonies)
"Spirit of America."
Includes bibliographical references (p.  ) and index.
Contents: The Narragansett people—Verrazano, Block, and Williams—The Rhode Island Colony—The American Revolution—The thirteenth state—Time line—Glossary terms.
  ISBN 1-56766-685-X (alk. paper)
  1. Rhode Island—History—Colonial period, ca. 1600–1775—Juvenile literature. 2. Rhode Island—History—1775–1865—Juvenile literature. [1. Rhode Island—History—Colonial period, ca. 1600–1775. 2. Rhode Island—History—1775–1865.] I. Title. II. Series.
  F82.S68 2003
  974.5'02—dc21                    2003003775

12                    20                    26

# *Contents*

# Chapter ONE

# The Narragansett People

*Wooly mammoths roamed the continent of North America thousands of years ago. They were hunted by the early Native Americans.*

ELEVEN THOUSAND YEARS AGO, NATIVE PEOPLE stalked woolly **mammoths** in what is now Rhode Island. Armed only with stone-tipped spears, they hunted the huge beasts, which weighed as much as today's elephants. They also gathered nuts, roots, and berries. These people had no permanent villages or homes. They constantly moved in search of the food they hunted. When an area no longer had mammoths or other large animals, the people looked for new hunting grounds.

Over time, native people in what is now Rhode Island began forming groups and building villages. They are called the Archaic people. They made stone tools for cutting and hunting. They fished in the streams and the bay. Archaic people hunted deer, moose, bear, and raccoon for meat and hides.

By 700 B.C., the Woodland people had replaced the Archaic people. Woodland groups hunted, fished, and farmed. They planted corn, beans, squash, and tobacco. They wove baskets for storing food and made clay pottery for cooking and holding liquids. The Woodland period lasted more than 2,000 years. During that time, Rhode Island's native population increased to around 30,000 people. The Narragansett, Rhode Island's main Native American group, are distant relatives of the Woodland people.

The Narragansett, like many Native Americans along North America's east coast, spoke a form of Algonquian. Having this

*Archaic people used simple stone tools, like these, for cutting and hunting.*

## Interesting Fact

▶ The Archaic people used hard stone such as flint and granite to make tools and weapons. They shaped knives and spear points by chipping down flint. Axes and tools for preparing food were often made of granite, which was then polished.

7

*The Narragansett Bay region was home to Rhode Island's main Native American group, the Narragansett.*

common language made it easy for Native Americans from Virginia to Canada to trade among themselves. The word Narragansett refers both to the native group and the place where they lived. The Narragansett lived near Narragansett Bay, which slices into what is now Rhode Island. Many Narragansett also lived on islands in the bay.

The Narragansett built winter and summer camps. Winter camps were set up in forests where game was plentiful. When spring came, the people moved to a summer camp. There, they planted crops, fished, and hunted. Extra corn, beans, and fish were dried and stored for the following winter.

8

Families lived in homes called wigwams. The wigwams were made of wooden frames covered with bark. Men hunted, fished, and made tools and weapons. The men also traded with other groups and protected the village from attack. Women worked the fields, collected food, and dried herbs for medicine. They cooked, cleaned, and cared for children. The children also helped out. They chased crows away from crops and picked fruit, berries, and nuts.

The Narragansett had no written language. They passed on their history through spoken tales and legends. The group's elders taught the children about Narragansett history.

The first known meeting between the Narragansett and Europeans took place in 1524. That year, Italian explorer Giovanni da Verra-

*Narragansett chief Ninigret, like other chiefs before him, was responsible for protecting his people and preserving their traditions.*

zano sailed into Narragansett Bay. The Narragansett people impressed Verrazano. He said, "This is the goodliest people and of the fairest conditions that we have found in this our voyage."

*Giovanni da Verrazano was born in Italy but explored North America for France. He was impressed by the Narragansett people when he encountered them in 1524.*

THE NARRAGANSETT THOUGHT THAT ALL LIFE CAME FROM CAUTANTOWWIT, their main god. They believed Cautantowwit tried first to create humans from a stone. This was not a success. He then created people from a tree. All humans came from these "second" people. Cautantowwit then sent a crow to give the Narragansett corn for planting. In this way, he provided food for his people.

The Narragansett believed that lesser gods, called manitous, held power over different parts of nature. Manitous controlled the sun, moon, water, fire, and wind. These gods provided such things as rain for growing crops and fire for cooking.

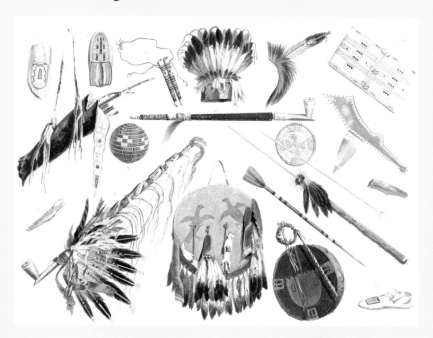

When a Narragansett died, relatives and friends buried the body with the important items of life. Food, pots, and spoons have been found in Narragansett graves, along with tobacco pipes and weapons. The bodies were dressed with beads, earrings, and necklaces.

Narragansetts grieved when they lost a family member. They blackened their faces with charcoal as a sign of mourning. The dead person's name was not spoken. People with the same name as the dead person took new names. Sometimes, 10 years or more would pass before the dead person's name would be used again.

# Chapter TWO

# Verrazano, Block, and Williams

*Vikings may have crossed the Atlantic in a longboat like this one. They may have seen Rhode Island as early as A.D.1000.*

VIKING OR IRISH EXPLORERS MAY HAVE SEEN the land that is now called Rhode Island as early as A.D. 1000. Historians know that both the Irish and the Vikings, who were from Norway, sailed in North American waters. These sailors left no records of their journeys, however.

Giovanni da Verrazano, who arrived in 1524, was the first European known for certain to have seen Rhode Island. He wrote a report to Francis I, the French king who paid for his trip. Verrazano said that he had "discovered an island in the form of a triangle, distant from the mainland ten leagues [about 30 miles or 50 kilometers], about the bigness of the Island of Rhodes." Verrazano's comments may have given Rhode Island its name.

In 1614, two other explorers sailed into the waters off present-day Rhode Island. The first was Englishman John Smith, who had helped establish a settlement in Virginia. The second was Dutch explorer Adriaen Block. Block visited an island in the ocean off Rhode Island. He named this island after himself, and it is still called Block Island today. Some people think Block gave Rhode Island its name. He called one of the islands in Narragansett Bay Roodt Eylandt, which means "red island" in English, because of its red soil. In Dutch, roodt is pronounced "road."

*Francis I, king of France, paid for Verrazano's exploration of North America.*

The first European to settle in Rhode Island was William Blackstone, an English minister who had been living in Boston, Massachusetts. Blackstone arrived in Rhode Island in 1635. He built a cabin on the banks of the a river that was later named for him.

In the winter of 1636, another minister named Roger Williams was forced to leave Massachusetts. The Massachusetts Bay Colony had been founded by **Puritans.** The Puritans had left England so they could practice their religion as they wished, but they did not allow other people religious freedom.

*Roger Williams was a minister who was forced to leave the Massachusetts Bay Colony because he believed in religious freedom for all, not just for the Puritans. When he arrived in Rhode Island, he was assisted by the Narragansett.*

Williams fled to Rhode Island with a handful of friends. By the time he got there, he was suffering from severe cold and frostbite. The Narragansett people cared for Williams until he regained his health. They also sold Williams land to build a settlement.

Williams and his friends founded the **Providence** Plantations, which in time became the center of the Rhode Island Colony. Williams chose the name Providence because he was grateful for "God's merciful providence" in leading him to a safe haven. Williams wanted everyone who lived in Rhode Island to enjoy freedom of religion.

Two years later, the Massachusetts Bay Colony forced Anne Hutchinson to leave Boston. Hutchinson was an outspoken Puritan who claimed that God helped her explain the Bible. She, her family, and a man named William Coddington headed south to find religious freedom. They founded the town of Portsmouth in 1638.

New settlements developed as more people

*Anne Hutchinson was a Puritan who openly criticized some Puritan religious ideas and leaders. She was forced to leave Boston because of her willingness to express her beliefs.*

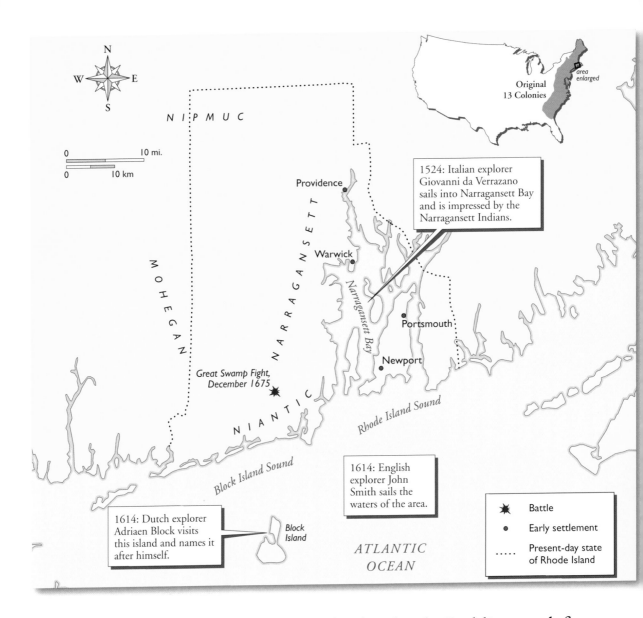

N

W    E

S

N I P M U C

0       10 mi.

0       10 km

Providence

M O H E G A N

N A R R A G A N S E T T

Warwick

Narragansett Bay

Portsmouth

Newport

Great Swamp Fight,
December 1675

N I A N T I C

Rhode Island Sound

Block Island Sound

Block
Island

ATLANTIC
OCEAN

1524: Italian explorer
Giovanni da Verrazano
sails into Narragansett Bay
and is impressed by the
Narragansett Indians.

1614: English
explorer John
Smith sails the
waters of the area.

1614: Dutch explorer
Adriaen Block visits
this island and names it
after himself.

Original
13 Colonies

area
enlarged

✴    Battle

●    Early settlement

·····    Present-day state
of Rhode Island

*Rhode Island Colony at the time of the first European settlement*

moved into Rhode Island. Coddington left Portsmouth to begin the town of Newport in 1639. Three years later, Samuel Gorton left Portsmouth to start a settlement that he called Warwick. Small villages also sprang up at Wickford and Pawtuxet.

16

Roger Williams was a Puritan minister who did not always follow Puritan ways. He believed in freedom of religion. Williams, who was born in 1604, moved from England to Massachusetts in 1631.

In Massachusetts, Williams became a friend of the Wampanoag people. He often spoke out against the Puritan practice of forcing Native Americans to become Christians. He believed native people should be free to follow their own religion. He said, "Forced worship stinks in God's nostrils." Williams also believed that English settlers should pay native people for their land. Such ideas were not popular with the Puritans.

In 1635, the Puritan leaders decided to force Williams to leave Massachusetts. They planned to put him on a boat back to England. Williams was warned in advance. He fled south to Rhode Island, where he knew the Narragansett chiefs Canonicus and Miantonomi. The Narragansett sold Williams the land that became the Providence Plantations.

Williams and his wife, Mary, raised their family in Providence. They had six children, named Mary, Freeborn, Providence, Mercy, Daniel, and Joseph. Roger Williams died in 1683. About 100 years later, Williams's idea of freedom of religion was enshrined in the U.S. **Constitution** as the guaranteed right of every American.

# Chapter THREE

# The Rhode Island Colony

*Touro Synagogue, the oldest Jewish house of worship in the United States, is located in Newport, Rhode Island. People of many different faiths settled in Rhode Island because of the religious freedom they found there.*

RELIGIOUS FREEDOM DREW PEOPLE OF MANY faiths to Rhode Island. The first Baptist church in the United States was organized in Providence in 1639. Roger Williams was its leader. Quakers settled on the island of Aquidneck in 1657. Jews came to Newport

in 1658. French Protestants settled in a town called East Greenwich.

Each of these religious groups brought new traditions and customs to Rhode Island. They provided doctors, lawyers, teachers, merchants, and skilled craftspeople to support town life.

At the center of each Rhode Island town was a meetinghouse. Town meetings were held in the meetinghouses, as were trials and government councils. Most towns had at least one church. Children learned their lessons in one-room schools. Livestock grazed on the village green, a grassy space in the middle of town. Townsfolk drew water from a town well. Wrongdoers were locked in stocks as punishment for their crimes. Stocks are wooden frames with holes for locking ankles and hands in place.

Newport, Providence, Bristol, and Warwick became active seaports as towns began trading with European coun-

*Interesting Fact*

▸ The oldest schoolhouse in the United States is located in Portsmouth, Rhode Island. It was built in 1716.

*A criminal in stocks was a common sight in New England towns. People believed that the shame would keep the criminal from committing more crimes.*

*Chief Metacomet was called King Philip by the English colonists. He led the Wampanoag in a war against the colonists to regain control of their land.*

## Interesting Fact

▶ The village blacksmith often also acted as dentist. He was usually the only one who had pliers—for pulling teeth!

tries. Seaport shops sold goods from England and France. Most towns had a cooper (barrel maker), a potter, a miller, a shoemaker, a carpenter, and a blacksmith.

For nearly 40 years, Rhode Island settlers and the Narragansett people remained friendly. Then, in 1675, that friendship ended. That year, a war began between white settlers in Massachusetts and the Wampanoag. In Rhode Island, the Narragansett had sold the white settlers their land. But in other colonies, settlers greedy for land simply forced the native people to move. The native people had also been devastated by diseases the Europeans had brought to North America. Finally, the Wampanoag people had had enough. They began to fight back in what is known as King Philip's War.

The Narragansetts did not want to take part in the war. Unfortunately, Wampanoag women, children, and wounded warriors arrived in the Narragansett winter camp near the Great Swamp. The Narragansetts offered food, shelter, and medical care to the Wampanoags. Rhode Island settlers knew the Narragansetts were protecting the Wampanoags. They attacked the Narragansetts in what is called the Great Swamp Fight. Nearly 700 Narragansetts died.

A few months later, the surviving Narragansett warriors attacked a group of English settlers. They also burned Providence. Though the Narragansett won some small battles, in the end they lost control of their land. They could not defeat the settlers.

By the mid-1700s, Rhode Island had become a profitable colony. Onions, dairy

*Though Native Americans won some battles in King Philip's War, in the end they lost control of their land and thousands of them lost their lives.*

*A Rhode Island farm house, built in the early 1700s*

products, livestock, and apples were produced on large farms worked by slave labor. Lumber mills turned out wood for building houses, furniture, and barrels. Fishing and whaling provided food and fuel oil.

Some Rhode Islanders made huge profits shipping goods to and from Europe. Piracy paid even better, since pirates sold goods they stole. Pirate ships were as common in Rhode Island ports as merchant ships. Rhode Island earned the nickname Rogues Island because of all the criminals found there. One minister called the colony "the sewer of New England."

FOR NEARLY 100 YEARS, RHODE ISLAND'S ECONOMY FLOURISHED FROM THE sale of human beings. Rhode Island's 421 slave ships sailed from Bristol, Newport, Providence, and Warren.

The colony developed a trade in slaves, molasses, and rum. Africans were captured or bought in their homeland. They were then sold in the Caribbean, where they worked as slaves in sugarcane fields. These fields produced molasses. Rhode Island merchants bought the molasses and used it to make rum. Money earned from selling rum paid for more voyages to collect slaves.

Some enslaved people were brought to Rhode Island. Between 1709 and 1807, more than 106,000 Africans were sold in Rhode Island's slave markets.

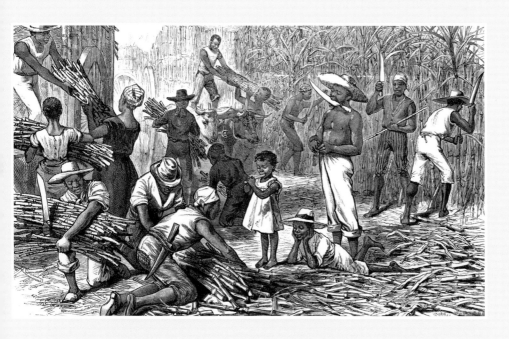

But not everyone in Rhode Island approved of slavery. The Quakers urged others to end the slave business. In 1774, Rhode Island banned bringing new slaves into the colony. Slave traders ignored the ban. Ten years later, the colony passed the **Emancipation** Act. This act freed all children of enslaved people born after March 1, 1784. By 1840, Rhode Island had only five slaves.

# Chapter FOUR

# The American Revolution

*The Mississippi River is the largest river in North America. At the end of the French and Indian War, England controlled all of what is now the United States east of the Mississippi River.*

MERCHANTS AND SHIPPERS WERE GROWING rich in Rhode Island during the 18th century. Farther west, England and France were arguing over the rich farmland and fur trade in the Ohio River valley. This conflict turned into the

French and Indian War, which was fought between 1754 and 1763. In the end, England gained all land east of the Mississippi River.

Fighting the French and Indian War proved very expensive for Great Britain. The British thought the American colonies should help pay off their war debt. So the British passed laws to raise money by taxing the colonists. Because the colonists did not send representatives to Parliament, Great Britain's lawmaking body, colonists talked against this "taxation without representation."

The Sugar Act of 1764 taxed cloth, coffee, wine, and sugar. The Stamp Act charged tax on all printed materials, from legal documents to playing cards. The Quartering Act required the colonies to feed and house British soldiers. In

THE

# RIGHTS

OF

# COLONIES

## EXAMINED.

Stephen Hopkins

PUBLISHED BY AUTHORITY.

PROVIDENCE:
PRINTED BY *WILLIAM GODDARD.*
M.DCC.LXV.

*Stephen Hopkins, the chief magistrate of the colony of Rhode Island, published this pamphlet to protest the Stamp Act and other British acts that required the colonists to pay taxes on many goods.*

many cases, soldiers lived in colonists' homes and ate with their families. The Townshend Acts of 1767 added taxes on glass, lead, paint, paper, and tea.

The Sugar Act hurt Rhode Island's profitable molasses-rum-slave trade. In 1769, the British ship *Liberty* blocked Newport Harbor. It prevented ships from **smuggling** molasses into Rhode Island without paying the sugar tax. Rhode Islanders solved the anti-smuggling problem. They burned the *Liberty*.

*Rhode Islanders rebelled against the British by setting fire to the* Liberty *and the* Gaspee *(below), two British ships that were interfering with the smuggling of goods into Rhode Island.*

Rebellion blossomed in Rhode Island. Three years later, Rhode Islanders dealt with a ship called the *Gaspee,* which was preventing the smuggling of paper goods. Burning the *Liberty* had proved successful, so Rhode Islanders set fire to the *Gaspee* as well.

In March 1775, colonists in Providence protested the tax on tea by dumping a ship's cargo into the harbor. By this time, most Rhode Islanders wanted nothing more to do with Great Britain. On May 4, 1776, Rhode Island declared independence from Great Britain, two months before the **Declaration of Independence** was signed.

Rhode Island provided soldiers, ships, and goods to help the American Revolution (1775–1783). The colony's Nathaniel Greene led the Continental army in the south.

*Nathaniel Greene was the commander of the Continental army in the southern United States.*

▶ The Colony House, in Newport, is the fourth-oldest state-house still in existence in the United States. It took about three years to build, from 1736 to 1739. During the years the British occupied Newport, they used the Colony House as a barracks to house soldiers.

*Esek Hopkins was the first commander in chief of the Continental Navy.*

Rhode Island's Black Regiment, a troop of African-American soldiers, fought under General Greene. It was the first all-black regiment in American history. Another Rhode Islander, Esek Hopkins, became the first commander of the Continental navy.

In December 1776, the British took over Newport. Then, in August 1778, American and French troops attacked the British at Newport. This was the first time American and French armies worked together. The Battle of Rhode Island ended with no real winner. A year later, the British decided to leave Newport. British troops were needed to support the war effort in the south.

*French ships enter the harbor at Newport, Rhode Island, in 1778. The attack on the British at Newport was the first time that the American and French forces worked together during the Revolutionary War.*

DURING THE AMERICAN REVOLUTION, the British had one big advantage over the colonists: They could travel by ship from colony to colony. The colonies had no navy—until Rhode Island formed one.

In 1775, Rhode Island's government agreed to pay for a navy. The first American navy consisted of two ships: the *Katy* and the *Washington.* The main goal of these ships was to stop a British ship called the *Rose,* which was preventing supply ships from landing in Rhode Island. Captain Abraham Whipple commanded the *Katy.* Whipple was happy to irritate the British by attacking supply ships that served the *Rose.*

In June 1775, the *Katy* met the British supply ship *Diana* in the first naval battle of the American Revolution. The *Katy* fired on the *Diana,* causing serious damage. After only half an hour, the *Diana* lay broken apart on the rocks of a nearby island. Its crew abandoned ship. Captain Whipple enjoyed the first victory of the American navy.

The *Katy* and the *Washington* never stopped the *Rose*. Eventually, the *Rose* headed south with the British troops. In 1779, the *Rose* sank off the coast of Savannah, Georgia.

Rhode Island's representative to the **Continental Congress** presented a plan to build a colonial navy. The Rhode Island plan called for the two ships it had to chase British trade vessels in North American waters. Congress would buy 13 more ships to form the new Continental navy. Because of Rhode Island's two-ship fleet, Narragansett Bay became known as the Cradle of the American Navy.

# Chapter FIVE

# The Thirteenth State

*Rhode Island sent no representatives to the Constitutional **Convention** in 1787. The U.S. Constitution was written at that historic meeting.*

WHEN THE AMERICAN REVOLUTION ENDED in 1783, the new states followed the **Articles of Confederation.** The articles were a group of laws that covered all states. But the articles were weak and gave little power to the central government. The U.S. Constitution replaced the Articles of Confederation in 1787.

Although Rhode Island was the first state to declare independence, it was the last to

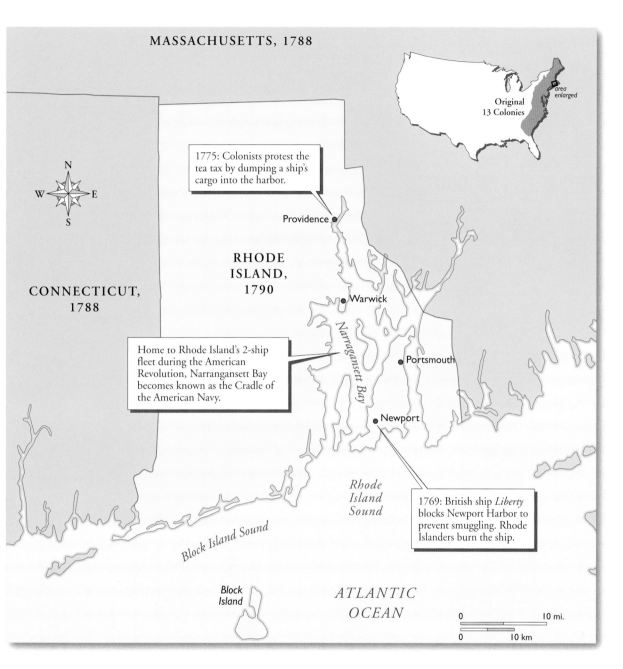

MASSACHUSETTS, 1788

Original
13 Colonies

area
enlarged

1775: Colonists protest the tea tax by dumping a ship's cargo into the harbor.

Providence

RHODE ISLAND, 1790

CONNECTICUT, 1788

Warwick

Home to Rhode Island's 2-ship fleet during the American Revolution, Narrangansett Bay becomes known as the Cradle of the American Navy.

Narragansett Bay

Portsmouth

Newport

Rhode Island Sound

1769: British ship *Liberty* blocks Newport Harbor to prevent smuggling. Rhode Islanders burn the ship.

Block Island Sound

Block Island

ATLANTIC OCEAN

0        10 mi.

0      10 km

approve the Constitution. Many Rhode Islanders did not want a strong federal government. They were afraid that the **federal** government would take away the

*Rhode Island Colony before statehood*

*The Newport Colony House was the site of the colonial government in Rhode Island and served as its state house until 1901.*

state's power to make its own decisions on issues such as slavery. Rhode Islanders, especially the state's Quakers, did not like what the Constitution said about slavery. Rhode Island had already passed a law banning slavery in 1784. Most Rhode Islanders did not want a Constitution that allowed slavery.

Farmers also opposed having a powerful federal government. They worried that the merchants would control the politicians and that the politicians would not understand the needs of farmers. Farm interests controlled the Rhode Island General Assembly, the state's

**legislature.** Eleven times, farm representatives prevented a meeting to review and approve the Constitution. Instead, Rhode Island held a general vote. Rhode Islanders rejected the Constitution by a vote of 2,708 to 237.

Finally, Rhode Island held a constitutional convention. By this time, the Bill of Rights had been added to the Constitution. The Bill of Rights is the first 10 amendments, or changes, to the Constitution. It protects individual rights, such as freedom of religion and freedom of speech.

Newspapers suggested that Rhode Islanders approve the Constitution because the federal government would help the state pay off its war debt. Rhode Island representatives approved the Constitution by a slim two-vote margin. The date was May 29, 1790. George Washington had already been president for a year when Rhode Island became the thirteenth state.

*George Washington is sworn in as the first president of the United States. By the time Rhode Island ratified the Constitution, George Washington had already been president for one year.*

**1524**   Giovanni da Verrazano sails near what is now Rhode Island.

**1614**   Dutch explorer Adriaen Block visits an island off of Rhode Island, which he names after himself.

**1635**   William Blackstone becomes the first European settler in Rhode Island.

**1636**   Roger Williams flees Massachusetts to form the Rhode Island Colony.

**1638**   Anne Hutchinson and William Coddington start the Portsmouth settlement.

**1639**   Coddington founds the Newport colony.

**1652**   African slaves are brought to Rhode Island for the first time.

**1675**   White Rhode Islanders battle the Narragansett in the Great Swamp Fight.

**1769**   The British ship *Liberty* is burned in Newport Harbor.

**1772**   Rhode Islanders burn the British ship *Gaspee.*

**1774**   Rhode Island bans bringing new slaves into the colony.

**1776**   Rhode Island declares independence from Great Britain. British troops take over Newport.

**1784**   Rhode Island passes the Emancipation Act, which frees children of slaves born after March 1, 1784.

**1790**   Rhode Island becomes the 13th state on May 29.

# *Glossary* TERMS

**Articles of Confederation (AR-ti-kuhls uhv kuhn-FED-ur-ay-shun)**
The Articles of Confederation was the first constitution for the United States. It was replaced in 1787 by the U.S. Constitution.

**constitution (kon-stuh-TOO-shun)**
A constitution is a written document that sets up a government. The U.S. Constitution came into affect in 1787.

**Continental Congress (kon-tuh-NIHN-tuhl KONG-griss)**
The Continental Congress was a meeting of colonists that served as the American government during the Revolutionary War. Each colony sent a number of representatives to the Congress.

**convention (kuhn-VEN-shuhn)**
A convention is a gathering of people who have the same interests, such as a political meeting. The Constitutional Convention gathered people from each colony to write the rules for the future government.

**Declaration of Independence (dek-luh-RAY-shuhn uhv in-di-PEN-duhnss)**
The Declaration of Independence is the document that declared the 13 colonies free from Great Britain. The Rhode Island Colony declared its independence two months before the Declaration was signed.

**emancipation (i-MAN-si-pay-shuhn)**
Emancipation is the act of setting someone or something free. Rhode Island emancipated its slaves in 1784.

**federal (FED-uh-ruhl)**
The federal government is the central or national government of a country. Each state has its own state government as well.

**legislature (LEJ-iss-lay-chur)**
A legislature is the group of people who have the power to make or change the laws of a state or nation. The Rhode Island Colony's legislature was called the General Assembly.

**mammoths (MAM-uhths)**
Mammoths were large, hairy animals the size of elephants. They lived during the Ice Age.

**providence (PROV-uh-denss)**
Providence is guidance from God. This word is the basis for the name of the Rhode Island Colony's capital.

**Puritans (PYOOR-uh-tuhns)**
The Puritans were early American colonists who wanted a "purer" form of religion than was practiced in England. Roger Williams was a Puritan minister who was forced to leave Massachusetts.

**smuggling (SMUHG-ling)**
Smuggling is the bringing of goods into an area illegally. Before the Revolutionary War, people were smuggling in goods to avoid paying taxes to the British.

# Rhode Island Colony's FOUNDING FATHERS

## John Collins (1717–1795)
Articles of Confederation signer; Continental Congress delegate, 1778–80, 1782–83; Rhode Island governor, 1786–90

## William Ellery (1727–1820)
Continental Congress, 1776–81, 1783–85; Declaration of Independence signer; Articles of Confederation signer; Rhode Island state supreme court justice, 1785

## Stephen Hopkins (1707–1785)
Continental Congress delegate, 1774–78; Declaration of Independence signer; Rhode Island general assembly member, 1777–79

## Henry Marchant (1741–1796)
Continental Congress delegate, 1777–79; Articles of Confederation signer; U.S. district court for Rhode Island justice, 1790–96

# *For Further* INFORMATION

## *Web Sites*

Visit our homepage for lots of links about the Rhode Island colony:
**http://www.childsworld.com/links.html**

*Note to Parents, Teachers, and Librarians:*
We routinely verify our Web links to make sure they're safe,
active sites—so encourage your readers to check them out!

## *Books*

Cox, Clinton. *Come All You Brave Soldiers: Blacks in the Revolutionary War.*
New York: Scholastic, 1999.

Furbee, Mary Rodd. *Outrageous Women of Colonial America.* New York: John
Wiley & Sons, 2001.

Gaustad, Edwin S. *Roger Williams: Prophet of Liberty.* New York: Oxford
University Press, 2001.

Hakim, Joy. *Making Thirteen Colonies.* New York: Oxford Press, 1999.

Harper, Judith E. *African Americans and the Revolutionary War.* Chanhassen,
Minn.: The Child's World, 2001.

Schlesinger, Arthur M. Jr., editor. *Anne Hutchinson: Religious Leader.*
Broomall, Pa.: Chelsea House, 2000.

## *Places to Visit or Contact*

### Rhode Island Historical Society
*To learn about the history and people of Rhode Island*
110 Benevolent Street
Providence, RI 02906-3103
401/331-8575

### Coggeshall Farm Museum
*To find out about all the hard work that went into colonial farming; this working
farm features farm animals, a barn, and a blacksmith's shop*
Colt State Park
Bristol, RI 02809
401/253-9062

# Index

## About the Author

BARBARA SOMERVILL IS THE AUTHOR OF MANY BOOKS FOR CHILDREN. She loves learning and sees every writing project as a chance to learn new information or gain a new understanding. Ms. Somervill grew up in New York State, but has also lived in Toronto, Canada; Canberra, Australia; California; and South Carolina. She currently lives with her husband in Simpsonville, South Carolina.